PRAYER ZONES
AND
TIME ZONES

2 Kings 7 vs 1

Reserved Copy Right 2016
ISBN
978-0-7974-7786-5

Preface

How many times have you asked yourself, how do I pray about every circumstance? When do I pray about it? What is happening around time zones and prayer zones? What are the appropriate prayer points on time zones and prayer zones? Why I am fainting in business, projects, connections, marriages, spiritual life, relationships.

This Prayer zones and Time Zones book will give you the prayer guideline, and spiritual insights enrichments on Time zones and faith to overcome every circumstance you are facing today. Learn how to express yourself freely in prayer, shows God's power on each prayer in each day and always avoid fainting through it all even to the spiritual life.

Introduction

The ingredients of my destiny, my goals, spiritual life, my visions, my health, my projects, my dreams, my success, my connections, my relationships, my spiritual and my physical footsteps, my money, are programmed into days, years and seasons.

I declare a spermatic word in mornings, afternoons and evenings that will make contact with the womb of my days, and make my years and seasons pregnant out. At midnight prayer zones, I declare prophetic declarations upon myself, at the darkest part of the night- middle of the night, I speak the proof of the armour of God and refuge of God at sunrise, the dawn will give birth to the will of God and the great light shall light shall direct the path of my declarations and bring fourth my daily bread, at the noon day my enemies will flee, and newly found spoils will await me at my destination, at financial zone my financial life is inevitable and I will be strategically lined up with the ladder of Angels of fortunes in business connections, relationships.

As I jump start the day commander and capture prayer zones and time zones, time is being redeemed. The spiritual airways and highways are being hijacked for Jesus. The atmosphere of the airways over my destiny, career, my family, my time zones, my business, and projects is producing a new climate.

Prayer Zone

Prayer is when humanity interacts with divinity and vice versa. Prayer is a mode of communication with God. Prayer goes beyond talking or interacting with God, its God releasing His mind to humanity. In order to understand God's communication with us, we must be diligent to read, to study, memorize and meditate on His word. Prayer qualifies us to receive answers from God. Prayer graduates us to receive instruction from God and hearing His voice. As we communicate with God the first part of that communication is listening. Trying to shortcut or excuse ourselves from prayer creates spiritual potholes it opens us up in road of the deception demons into our minds and deception of our own fallen nature. Prayer directs towards a diety, spirit, lofty ideas for the purposes of worshiping (adoration), confession (of specific sin), thanksgiving (gratitude), supplication (specific request). Therefore belief is the backbone of prayer, thus one should believe God is actually listening to his prayers and he is certain will receive the desired results. And the route of the fulfilment of the right desires demands prayer.

Time Zone

These are regions of the globe that observe a uniform or standard time for, legal commercial and social purposes. Therefore time zones observe what we do per each second, minute and hour to meet the desired results in your day. It involves what we speak and do which gives the divine behaviour. Everything we don't have is a reflection …. Of the time that has been taken away from us. Time is the only perfect gift which contains a distinctive deposit from God. Everything we fail to receive is a result of unwillingness to exchange for it. Therefore your goals give value on how you spend time on earth. If you don't know how to use your time well, somebody else can waste your time and create events for you.

Spiritual Clock

Spiritual Clock describes natural men in the physical world as it, illustrates with ordinary clock which comprises, of Spirit as second hand, soul as minute hand and body as hour hand. It gives full explanation of components which operate in a day.

There is a control zone which state both the mind of God and devil controlling a day. At control zone God designed each day for humanity to have domain and endure every promise. But the devil at control zone prescribes people to rejection and condemnation through influence to sin. God gives us provision to sin-free, peace and eternal life in Jesus Christ. Jesus Christ is the perfect will of God in action. Satan is the deceiver of brethren that influence people to into demonic oppression. In every human life there are two spiritual ladders that operate either to suppress or to give desired results.

There is a ladder of Angels which are ministering spirits that God assigned to serve us. Angels act on God's word that we speak out of our mouths. They listen to us speaking God's word and as we speak God's word, Angels rush to perform it in our lives.

The ladder of demons has devil ministers waiting for the opportunities to attack us and cause confusion in our daily activities. Demons don't have a physical body but they come and posses physical body or objects when we open doors for them and we have the right and power to dismiss them through our own willingness. Normally demons use our weakness to manipulate into our spiritual life. As the bible indicates in the book of Ecc 10:8 It says he who breaks the hedge invites a snake to come and bite him.

Wall clock shows environments where we take ourselves in the day. The law of environment is very important, because every environment natures our strength or weakness. If you go into a wrong environment the weakness will flourish and strength dies. Reflection colour of the clock inside describe how you will be visible on earth. This can only be reflected by the acceptance of Jesus Christ.

For your life, dreams, plans per day to be meaningful you must have Jesus Christ. The day we are born on earth we are just existing but the day we get born again we receive life. Any miracle you want to get outside Jesus Christ is divination. Jesus is our standard on how to live on earth. The clock must have a battery that gives energy and positive and negative terminals. In every situation has two voices, the voice of God or the voice of devil. The positive is the voice of God that is in every situation in order to bring elevation. And the negative is the voice of the devil that brings temptation in order to accuse or condemn.

The numbers on the clock are the goals and values that you undertake to pursue in every time zone. The quality of your life is revealed by the quality of instructions you choose to pursue. No matter how carefully you plan your goals they will never be more than pipe dreams unless you pursue them with gusto.
The kingdom of God gives grace, life and permanent solutions in everything we do in life but in the kingdom of devil there is a temporal solutions which leads to sorrowful and defeated life.

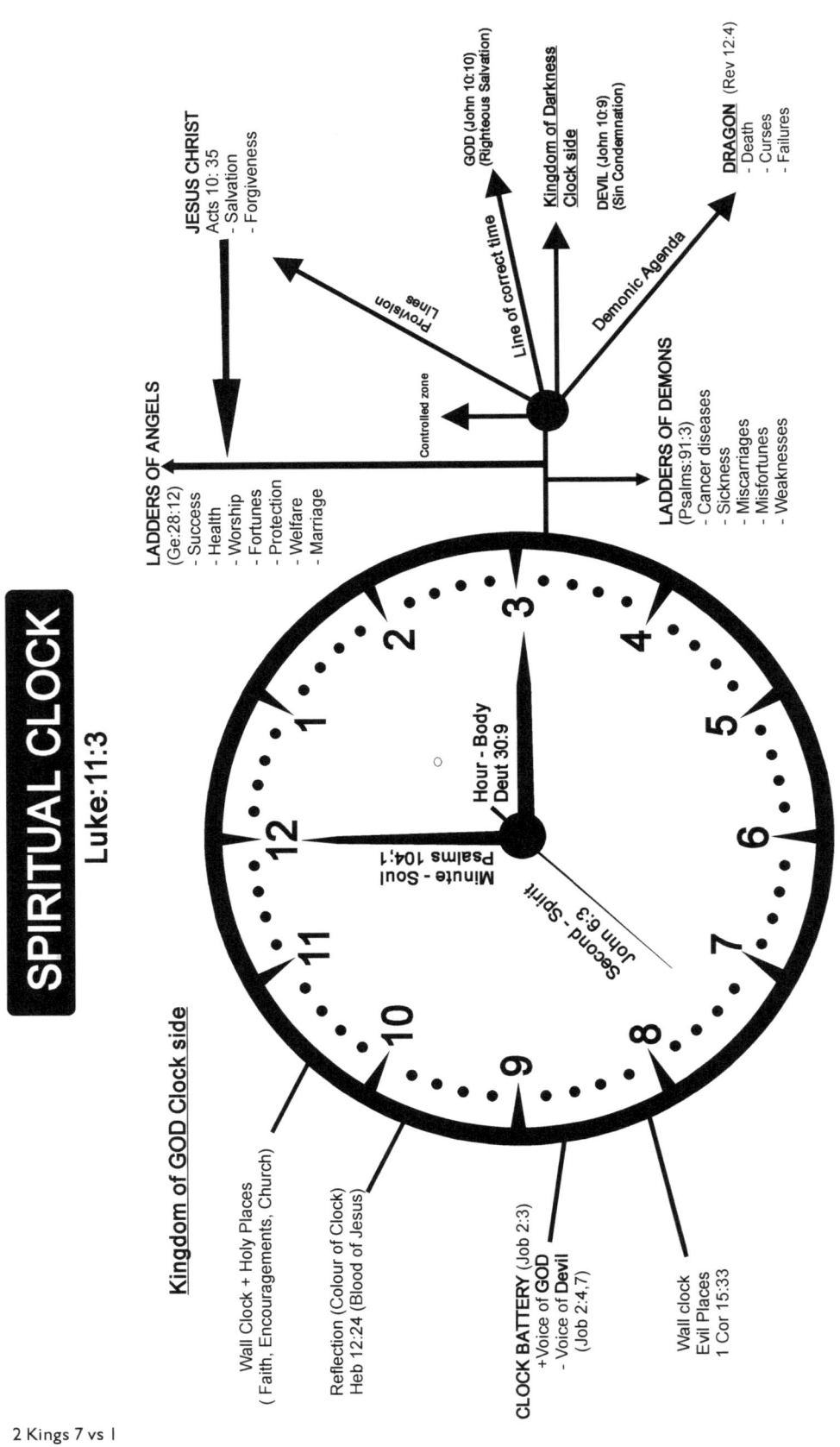

Attributes of the kingdom of God in controlling the day

John 3:16 *For God so loved the world, that he gave HIS only begotten Son, that whosoever believeth in HIM should not perish, but have everlasting life.*

Jesus is the greatest gift of humanity in spiritual and physical needs and healing, therefore it is manifested in our lives when we receive HIM and call upon HIS name. psalms 103:3-5

- Remission and forgiveness of sins, *Revelations 3:2; 1 John 1:9*
- Eternal life, *John 3:16; 1 John 5:11*
- Physical healing, *Matthew 8:17; 1 Peter 2:24*
- Emotional peace and restoration, *Psalms 23:1; Isaiah 26:3*
- Financial provision, *Psalms 23:1; Psalms 34:10*
- Wisdom, *1 Corinthians 1:30*
- Safety, *Psalms 91:11-12*
- Prosperity, *Psalms 1:3; 3 John 2*

Attributes of the Kingdom of darkness in controlling the spiritual clock

John 10:10 The thief cometh not, but for to steal, and to kill and to destroy: I am come that they might have life and that they might have it more abundantly.

- Malice, bitterness, unforgiving spirit and hatred
- Gossip and slander
- Talkativeness
- Abusiveness and cursing(anti-marriages, failures, poverty etc)
- Superiority \inferiority complex
- Tribal bigotry and racism
- Self –will, stubbornness and pride
- Suspicion and lack of trust
- Spirit of stealing and forgery
- Deceiving spirits and false hood
- Slothfulness ,lack of zeal, gluttony
- Violent, temper and impatience, lack fortitude
- Spirit of incest, lesbianism, sex with animals, homosexuality, and any form lusts
- Anger, wrath and rage

THE PRAYERFUL PERSON TRIANGLE AND LUKEWARM PERSON TRIANGLE

The bible in the book of Luke 18:1, Jesus said men ought always to pray and not to faint. Whenever men prays he boosts the supernatural men and natural men. Prayer keeps them alive and consistent in daily life but when they fail to pray everything around them goes down, the business, marriage, relationships, connections, spiritual life and the character. Prayerlessness will create the inroads of demonic attacks in life.

PRAYERFUL PERSON SUCCESS TRIANGLE ROMANS 8:26

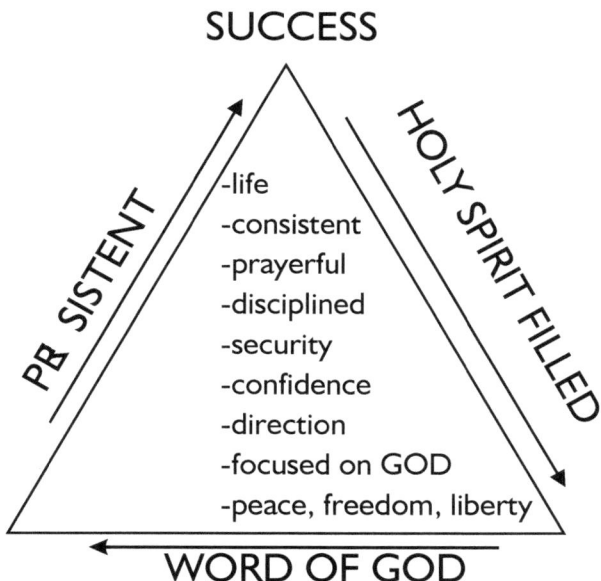

LUKEWARM PERSON FAILURE TRIANGLE Rev 3:15-16

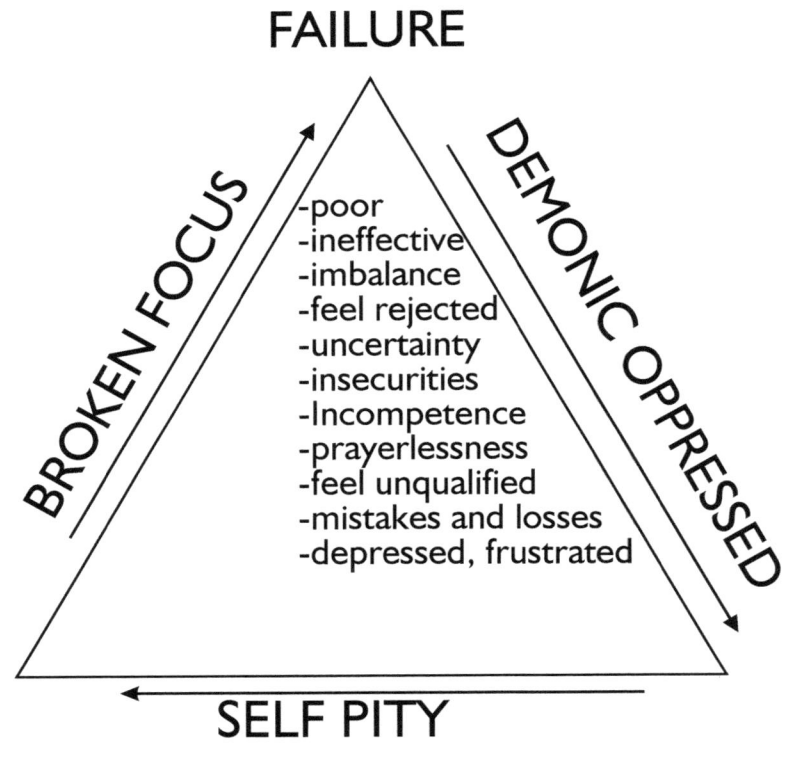

The Prayer Zones and time zones that control a day in a spiritual clock

1. Prayer zone: Declaration zone for the new day has started and speak good words on the new day and apply wisdom of God in pursuing dreams.
(Christ is your wisdom)

Time zone: 00:00AM - 01:00AM

But of Him are yea in Christ Jesus, who of God is made unto us wisdom and righteousness and sanctification and redemption.
1 Corinthians 1:30 KJV

When you depend on the Lord's wisdom to succeed, you see whatever you do prosper as we can see from the gospel how Our Lord Jesus flowed in divine wisdom in His earthly ministry.

In everything Jesus did, He was altogether lovely; He was never early never too late. He was always in perfect peace and never stressed or harassed. When it was time to tender, He was infinitely gentle, gracious and forgiving- we see this from His responses to the woman caught in adultery. When it was time to overturn the tables of moneychangers, He did it with passion. He was never puzzled by the Pharisees' attempts to trip Him and was always flowing with divine wisdom.

Beloved, begin to see yourself in Christ, who is always flowing with divine wisdom, always in control of the situation, and the same wisdom that flows in Him will flow in and through you. Purposing your new day with utterance of words of wisdom to your new day, no matter what the previous day skims against your destiny.

Prayer Strategy

- Listing down the things that you want to do during the day
- Opens the day with thanks giving prayer.

Prayer

Heavenly Father in the name of Jesus Christ, take me to the place where I am away from my pride, arrogance, failures, disappointment, discouraged and where Christ's humility is the centre stage , where I am lifting up holy hands and a pure heart to you in Jesus' name.

Mantle my physical and spiritual footsteps to the place where am no longer looking at the challenges, problems, mountains I face today, but to look down upon them, let the power of the holy ghost give me wisdom to execute my plans, dreams, projects, and business in Jesus' Name. Holy Spirit help me to see clearly and let my decisions be flooded with the light, truth and justice in Jesus name. Amen.

Declaration

I receive the wisdom of God in the market place, I have new sightseeing, and my destiny has the light of Jesus Christ. Today I have the energy of God upon my resolutions of the day. My heart is open to receive eternal wisdom. My ears are open for the Counsel of Holy Spirit, I receive the adoption of God's wisdom whereby I cry Abba Father in everything I plan to do today. I receive ordination of God's wisdom today to plan well, walk straight, discern, and recognise differences.

Scriptures

James 3:17; Romans 8:19; James 1; Psalms 119:62; Exodus 31:3, Proverbs 1:3; Proverbs 3:19; Proverbs 3:27; Proverbs 8:14; Ecclesiastes 10:10; Isaiah 11:2; Mark 6

2. Prayer zone: <u>Warfare zone</u>

Victories are not by accident but it's about fighting the right way. Behind every battle you must formulate good strategy to counter the enemy. What is your battle plan with the scriptures? Lots of people don't know how to fight the right way and gather the right resources for every battle. At this time zone witches take advantage of deep darkness and call the period witching hour. Witches fight against prosperity, health, wealth, opportunities, life and success, progress and future for next generation.

Time zone: 02:00AM -04:00AM

Spiritual warfare

Ephesians 6:11-12 Put on the whole armour of God that yea may be able to stand against the wiles of the devil.

For we wrestle not against flesh and blood, but against the rulers of the darkness of this world, against spiritual wickedness in high places.

Paul speaks of the power which comes from being equipped by God for the battle. The spiritual body armour will equip the soldier so that he can stand firm in the fight and the intense, close- quarters battle wrestling, while we may be tempted and tried through other human beings. But we must intent to identify the real source of the conflict.

Every component in the armour of God is important because we can use this strength and power against the "wiles of the devil". The devil has many methods but we are able to stand against his diabolical strategies when we put on the whole armour of God and the gospel has provided peace which equips us with the spiritual footing. The evil one wants to destroy our hope and diminish our convictions, but the shield of faith will quench all his fiery darts. But we must raise our faith and believe what God reveals and do what the Lord requires.

Beloved, Satan will tempt us to look down upon the importance of salvation, he likes us to think of it as a past experience only, however Paul encourages us to recall and consider the meaning of salvation, we are saved by the grace of God through faith and therein we stay. We have a power to demolish the evil schemes of the devil, you will not surely die, and the devil lied. Therefore we need to fasten on the seat belt of truth.

Prayer Strategy

- Write down the names of your family members, children, business etc. before you start praying and cover them with the blood of Jesus as you are praying.
- Go to a secret place where you conduct your prayers
- Itemizing every area when you pray and address it one by one

- Step on on your right feet to the things written on the paper that you don't want in your life as you cancel them violently in Jesus name
- Erecting altar offering after prayer and present it to the main altar in the church sessions

Prayer

Father in the name of Jesus Christ by the authority of Holy Ghost, I bind all the evil spirits, powers, entities in my family blood group, strongholds associated with evil spells against my life today in Jesus' name.

Every evil spell that is taking advantage of this darkest hour on this time zone to cast incantations of misfortunes' failures, abortions, disappointments, discouragement, missed opportunities, circle of negativity in my life, I silence and reverse it in Jesus Christ's name.

I dismantle every evil alter, alters of barrenness, generational curses, anti-marriages, anti-progress spirit, broken relationships, broken marriages, social spirits, foul spirit of death, these alters which have erected against my life, marriage, relationships, connections, business, projects and my career, be broken in Jesus' name.

I cause commotion to any demonic law that has been assigned to attack my life, my destiny, my marriage to lose its jurisdiction now in

Jesus' name, and every embargo of the enemy which have been placed in the area of my assignment to be uprooted now in Jesus' name.

Declaration

I renounce the shield of faith and I receive the covering of God upon the words I speak, my projects, my business, my career, my marriage, my relations, connections, in Jesus' name. I have the truth of Jesus Christ and His power that nothing by any means will hurt everything that I am doing today from the camps of the wicked because Christ in me, Christ behind me, Christ above me, and I abide in Jesus Christ forever by the power of faith.

Additional Scriptures

2 Thessalonians 2:10; 13
2 Timothy 2:4
Ephesians 6; Luke 10:19; Psalms 109

3. Prayer zone: Sunrise Zone: The activities of the day are established in these zones, during this time we hijack the airways of the morning to declare the prosperity of our days. The only trumpet of poverty is when a poor man do nothing

Time zone: 05:00AM-07:00AM

Call fourth what you want to see

………… *God, who gives life to the dead and calls those things which do not exist as though as they did* - **Romans 4:17**

How does God respond to our problems: For example how He addressed the issue of darkness? (Responded to the problem of darkness) The Bible tells us that when God saw darkness on the face of the deep, He said, "let there be light", and there was light as according to the book of Genesis 1:3. And God saw that it was good. He saw the good after He spoke. He didn't speak about the darkness He saw, instead, He spoke forth what He wanted to see.

God wants us to deal with the problems in our lives by speaking fourth what we want to see. Because the power to rule over the day has been given to greater light which is the sun as referenced by the first chapter of Genesis, I have seen many Christian communities waiting for the sunrise and speaking to the sun to deliver what they want to see their daily activities.

Now, I am not telling you to deny that your problem exists, but the darkness was there and God saw it, but He did not speak about what He saw. Rather, God chose to speak fourth what He wanted to see.

In fact, He called fourth everything of creation – the sun, moon, stars and animals, sea creatures and vegetation by simply speaking; He brought all these incredible things into existence.

Beloved, if you want to see good, then speak the good connections, relationships, business, best husband, wife, spiritual growth, that you want to see. Say decoration of favour of God upon your marriage, in the market and in your domain.

Prayer Strategy
Name the type of business that you want to see life in the day
Withhold company documents, curriculum vitae, important documents and speak light that bring manifestations on those documents

Prayer
Father in the name of Jesus Christ, I speak excellence and manifestation of your glory in this day. Let this day be filled with the power of the Holy Spirit. I pray that I function from a vantage position of boldness, audacity, victory in Jesus' name.

I pray that as the sun rises it shines upon my life wherever

I go and I pray that I won't struggle but I enjoy a blissful life of success and unending streams of miracles in this day in the name of Jesus. Amen

Declaration:
I go out with joy and I am led fourth with the peace of Jesus Christ in my work place, business, relationships, projects and my career. My steps are ordered of the Lord. Joy, health, peace, prosperity and the good tidings are in my life are the heritage of Christ.

Additional scriptures
Matthew 8:26, Matthew 9:29, Romans 14:11

4. Prayer zone: Decision Making Zone

Everyday a sea of decisions stretches before us some are small others large but they have larger impact on the day. Your decision create your income, gain, wealth, or losses in the day. We have to study market trends and make wise decisions in planning. At this time zone, the time is confused changing from morning to noonday and a lot of unwise decisions will spoil the rest of the day.

Time zone: 08:00AM-11:45AM

Smart people follow Jesus

Psalms 23:2
He makes me to lie down in green pastures; He leads me besides still waters.

In fact the world says, "He who fails to plan, plans to fail". You have got to make smart, detailed plans to succeed in life. You have got to study market trends and be in the knowhow, so that you can be that early bird that catches the worm. You also have got to keep looking over your shoulder because you never know when your competitors are going to catch up with you.

Is that how God wants you to live your life? Life of impoverishment, failure, hatred, murmurings, sorrows, depressed? Most certainly not! He wants you to be successful, peaceful, simply follow His good leading and He will lead you to a successful life.

Beloved, by all means, make plans and be diligent to know what you need to know in the field of your industry and in the areas where you are going to make important decisions. But first, seek and hear what Jesus is saying to you as you bring your concerns and what you need Him to do. Believe that He will lead you by His spirit and with His wisdom and perfect timing. And He will lead you to good success in ways beyond anything that you can ever plan for.

Prayer Strategy

Conduct the prayers with the employees before opening the business
Place every sample of products that you are selling in prayer room/secret place
Lay your hands to every item as you declare favour to them to be attractive to customers

Prayer

Heavenly Father in the name of Jesus Christ, I pray that when the sun rises in that day, as it is written in your word that you gave power to the sun to rule over the day and to bring a greater light in it. I speak that as it rise let notable victories and greater achievements be recorded in my area of dominion in Jesus' name.

I make the manifestation of the light of Jesus Christ and God's knowledge in every place, in my business, projects, marriage, connections. And let the reigning of Christ and bring Him glory today. Amen

Declaration

The light of Jesus Christ in this day is bringing glory and manifestation in whatever I am doing today. My day is receiving manifold wisdom, supernatural blessing, and revelation of God's word. I live above sickness, poverty, failure, death, defeat, and destruction in Jesus' name.

Additional scriptures

Hebrews 4:12; 2 Corinthians 2:14; Isaiah 55:10-11; 1 Corinthians 12:3; Philemon 1:6; Genesis 1:3

-

5. Prayer zone: Business Traffic Zone

Being busy is not measured by unnecessary movements you do, chatting, unnecessary meetings but it's measured by the quality of things you do in every minute which is characterised by the goals and values. If you are not selling something you are not in business. On this time zone, business absorbs market share, generate more sales, quick profit returns, fast moving products.

Time zone: 12:30PM-13:00PM

Give Jesus something to multiply

So he who had received five talents came and brought five of other talents, saying, "Lord, you delivered to me five talents, look, I have gained five more talents besides them".

His Lord said to him, "well done, good and fruitful servant".
Matthew 25:20-21

In the parable of the talents, the master commended the first two servants because they multiplied the money entrusted to them. They did not laze around drinking tea, complaining about how hard it is to get a job in this economy. On the contrary, they diligently, wisely and prudently found ways to double the money that had been entrusted to them. The Lord congratulated them and called them faithful servants.

Beloved, I have seen lots of chain prayers done by the intercessors leading them into a den of poverty, because they rely on praying only without doing anything. I want to encourage you to be a diligent, wise, good and faithful steward of the ideas, business, projects, money that God encourage you to be a diligent, wise, good and faithful steward of the ideas, business, projects, money that God has placed in your hands. As you trust the Lord for His provision, spend money to spend out your resumes, to go for interviews or even upgrade yourself for a better job. Don't bury money in the ground by sitting at home and watching television. Give Jesus a reason to multiply.

Prayer Strategy

Be alert and identify the products that customers are likely to buy

Prayer

Father in the name of Jesus, I ask for uncommon favour to those whom you have assigned to bring the blessing of my destiny. I decree that I sell profitable today, I command angels to stationed around my business to direct customers in the name of Jesus, let the oil of Your favour come upon me and let it never dry up, Your divine advertisement, divine promotion locate my business in Jesus name, may the angels of prosperity begin to touch my business and bring funds to me today. Every good thing presently eluding my business should begin to flow into it in Jesus name. I thank you for an ever increasing anointing of overflow in my business in Jesus' name. AMEN

Declaration

My business life is established with prosperity today in Jesus Christ's name. Amen. The foundation of whatever I do with my hands is strengthened upon the word of God in the name of Jesus Christ of Nazareth.

Additional scriptures

Deuteronomy 8:18, Matthew 25:20, Gensis 39:1-3, Gensis 21:23, Isaiah 48:17, Psalm 1:1-3, Psalm 35:27, Psalm37:3-7

6. Prayer zone: Financial Zone

The road to financial discipline, recovery, peace begins when you know how to handle every dollar that comes your way. Your willingness to pursue financial mentors who give advice on how to survive in financial crisis and build financial empire. At this zone know how best you place it into right accounts, daily deposits and profit making opportunities.

Time zone: 14:00 PM-16:00 PM

Deposit it in His Hands

And Jesus took the loaves, and when He had given thanks He distributed them to the disciples, and the disciples to those sitting down and likewise of the fish, as much as they

wanted. So when they were filled, He said to His disciples, "Gather up the fragments that remain, so that nothing is lost". Therefore they gathered them up and filled twelve baskets with fragments of the five barley loaves which were left over by those who had eaten.
John 6:11-13

In every business to flourish, you have to know and understand on how to deposit in order to get multiplication. This boy had five loaves and two little fish, but managed to feed five thousand men, (not counting the women and the children.) Not only were the people fed and till they were satisfied, there were also twelve baskets of left over. God bless you and provides abundantly for you and your family so that you can always find yourself in a position to give and be a blessing. Do not succumb to unwise borrowing. Do not take up easy credit loans which make available to you thousands of dollars (that are not yours to spend, and then struggle just to pay off the high interest late. Be also in a position to erect financial alters to attract sales volumes.

Beloved, be wise look to Christ for your provision and by His grace be diligent in all that you cannot help but be a blessing. Bring your little to Jesus Christ He will multiply whatever you place in His Hands with plenty left over. Let it be your daily habit that your business will have daily deduction in paying tithe whatever you earned a day.

Prayer strategy

Pray this at the spot of your business premises

You may anoint all your articles of trade and business premises if led by the holy spirit to do so

Lay your hands on as many trade items as possible for this prayer everyday

Pay your tithes promptly and give generous offering

Erecting financial alters for your business breakthrough

Prayer

Father in the name of Jesus Christ I thank you for gracing whatever I was doing today, I thank the word of God that has stored up in my heart and I thank you for your glory which produce results in my business, in my marriage and every area of my life today. As I am erecting these financial alters towards my business, marriage, relationship, connections today, I speak to be energised for victory, success, transformed from glory to glory in Jesus Christ's name.

Declaration

By the reason of this alter offering I speak my business to be renewed and well established transactions of God's favour in the market. From now on ,I receive divine wisdom for business management in Jesus name.

Additional scriptures

John 6:11; Joshua 1:8; 1 Timothy 4:15 ,
Deuteronomy 28:3-13, Psalm 1:1-3, Psalm 55:11,
Gensis 39:3, Joshua 1:8, Philippians 4:19,
11 Chronicles 20:20, Nehemiah 2:9, 111 John 2,
Job 22:28, Job 36:11, Colossians 2:4, 1 Samuel 30:8

7. Prayer zone: Forgiveness zone:

When the sun sets often they brought the sick to Jesus to be healed when the sun went down. Most people they overcome by the day – day activities and then into depression, self denial, sleepless nights.

Time zone: 18:30PM – 23:00PM

Keep your eyes on Jesus

Love has been perfected among us in this world as He is, so are we in the world.

When you look at yourself, your weaknesses and your negative circumstances, it is easy to become seized with anxiety, fear and despair. That is why God wants us to look at Jesus. In God's eyes because He has placed Christ Jesus' reality in our reality today as He is, so are we in this World.

So do not focus on your vulnerability or lack in your life and get discouraged. Ask yourself: Is Jesus abandoned, forgotten, sick or poor today? No He is at the right Hand of the Father, full of life, joy peace and favour. All of heaven's resources are at His disposal; He is greatly blessed, highly favoured and deeply loved by the father today, so are you.

To be likened to Jesus, to see as God sees. And when you see as God sees, you will also see the grace and supply of the Lord swallow up every lack in your life.

Prayer Strategy

Take action
Place the right hand on the area which is painful as you pray
Get rid of what caused the sickness and find solution by confessing sins and accepting Jesus Christ as your personal saviour

Prayer

Father in the name of Jesus Christ, give me the strength to take advantage of your grace and mighty power to fulfil my destiny in you. I am growing continually energised, from strength to strength, by your spirit in my inner man, my light is breaks forth as the morning and my health springs forth speedily and every organ, every tissue and every cells of my body will begin to function in the perfection which God created them to function in Jesus' name, Amen.

Declaration

I have God's energy upon my life today, whatever I suffered from; I am receiving abundant healthy life. I have the manifold of the peace of God in my house and the righteousness of Jesus Christ is perfecting my relationships today in Jesus Christ's name.

Additional scriptures

2 Corinthians 3:16, Hebrews 4:16, Psalm 20:6, Jeremiah 1:12, Numbers 23:19, Isaiah 53:5, 1Peter 2:24, Galatians 3:13,1 Corinthians 6:19-20, Exodus 15:26, Mathew 18:18, Romans 8:11, 1 Peter 1 :23, Psalm 107:20

Prayer of Salvation

Heavenly Father, I come before you, I accept that I am a sinner, I have sinned against you in deeds, in thoughts, forgive me. Father I ask the the blood of Jesus to wash my sins, cleanse me and sanctify me in Jesus' Name. Jesus I confess with my mouth that I accept you as my Lord and Saviour today. Amen.

Thank you for abiding in me, as I am abiding in you and write my name in the book of life, In Jesus' Name. Amen.

Conclusion

The proper use of prayer zone and time zone is determined by your willingness to study the word of God, meditate on scriptures investing time in prayer every day, developing daily life code, set the dominant goal of your day, and decisions to lavage on God's favour in a day.

Contact details
Head Quarters

Zimbabwe: +263 77 137 1716
America: +1(469) 835 - 0926
France: +33 6 40 29 55 93
south Africa: +27 61 451 0880
Angola: +244 923 550 238

www.ingramcontent.com/pod-product-compliance
Lightning Source LLC
Chambersburg PA
CBHW042116040426
42449CB00002B/61